Father's Day 2011

Dear Brad,

Not sure why this book title came "flying" into my mind but when the thought "arrived" I acted on it!

We all have times during our life that seem to be going the wrong way, plans spoiled or out of whack, etc. and it can be really frustrating.

This little book is an easy, interesting read and helps in understanding and getting through those times. Hope you (Dack Yi, too) enjoy having it as a reference. I know I have!

Much love,
Mom (Dad, too)

Steven Lane Taylor is a modern day sage. Beautifully written, his wonderful book shows us how living life in the divine flow is remarkably empowering.

~ Lissa Coffey, author of *What's Your Dosha, Baby?*

Today my life is filled with opportunities that I used to miss because I wasn't paying attention. Thank you, Steven, for showing me how to follow divine guidance and row with the flow.

~ Mary Ann Leslie, creator of I AMfirmations

Row, Row, Row Your Boat is simple and concise, yet it delivers a profound and impactful message. This is a book I will be sharing with friends, family, and clients alike.

~ Joy Malumphy, editor, Arizona Good Life News

I was astonished at the results I experienced when I applied the principles Steven describes so poignantly. Thank you, Steven, for this handbook to a more joyful and fulfilling life!

~ Janet White, author of *Secrets of the Hidden Job Market*

What theologians have made difficult, Steven Taylor has made simple and comprehensible. He has a great gift, and you will receive it when you read this book.

~ Reverend Christopher Ian Chenoweth
Founder of PositiveChristianity.org

ENDORSEMENTS

From the practical application of love
source of happiness, Steven Lane Taylo
densed great Truths into ordinary term:
profit greatly from reading and receiving t
of these pages.

~ FRANK AND MARGARET POUNDERS
Unity Church of Christianity,

Row, Row, Row Your Boat helped me s
of my job as a chance to live my dream.
one step at a time, and allowing myself
have been able to build a successful busine
struggle or undue stress. I am joyful ag
things are happening, and I am having fu

~ JAMIE HOEMANN, former advertis
Creator of 1

Steven has given us a practical and gent
reaching our destinations in life—one
beautifully. This is a man who has persor
every turn on life's river, and has become
pilot for us all.

~ MICHAEL A. MADAY, editor,

Through delightful stories of everyday li
Taylor makes this inspiring book a fun read
a practical guidebook for reaching your hig

~ DR. NANCY C. REEVES, psychologist a
I'd Say Yes, God, If I knew Wha

Row, Row, Row
Your Boat

ROW, ROW, ROW YOUR BOAT

A Guide for Living Life in the Divine Flow

STEVEN LANE TAYLOR

BROWN BOOKS PUBLISHING GROUP
DALLAS, TEXAS

Row, Row, Row Your Boat
© 2008 by Steven Lane Taylor
Printed and bound in the United States of America
Cover photograph by Cosmo Condina
Author's photograph by Marla McDonald

For information, please contact:
Brown Books Publishing Group
16200 North Dallas Parkway, Suite 170
Dallas, Texas 75248
www.brownbooks.com
972-381-0009
A New Era in Publishing™

ISBN-10: 0-9744597-3-9
ISBN-13: 978-0-9744597-3-8
LCCN 2003114923
2 3 4 5 6 7 8 9 10
First Printing, 2004
Second Printing, 2006
Third Printing, 2008

To Carol,
whose continual loving support
has been a constant reminder of the
unending flow of God's goodness.

CONTENTS

PREFACE

A number of years ago I was in Los Angeles, California, on a business trip. The hotel in which I was staying was hosting a convention at the time. I wasn't part of that convention, but I certainly could identify with its theme. For there, in the middle of the hotel lobby, stood a very large sign with these three words emblazoned upon it in bright blue letters: MAKE IT HAPPEN!

Make it happen. To me, those three words were much more than one company's war cry for the week. To me, those three words were the motto of my life. For I had always believed that if I wanted to get anything in particular out of life, then it was up to me—and me alone—to make it happen.

The way I saw it, the world wasn't out to do me any favors. Nothing came easy. And nothing came for free. And to put my faith in anyone or anything other than myself? Well, that seemed foolish to me. Whatever the goal, the only way to achieve success, I thought, was through hard work, determination, and, above all, control.

What a set-up for disappointment and frustration that was! I believed that I had to be in control of my life, yet nothing seemed to be in my control. I was consistently thwarted in my efforts to achieve the exact outcomes I desired. No matter how carefully I planned something, or how hard I worked to *make it happen,* it sometimes seemed as if the whole world was working against me. And even when I did manage to force things to go the way I wanted them to go, my victories were often hollow—hard won and hardly worth the effort. Or worse, my triumphs would set up a whole new set of problems. Life began to feel like one long, losing battle.

Then one afternoon I was working on an advertising project with my partner, Randee, and she got angry with me because I was once again second-guessing her work and trying to force things to go my way. "You know, Steve," she said, "your way is not the only way. It's just a different way. You don't have all the answers. And you don't always know what's best. You need to let go and let me do my job."

It was not the first time that I had been confronted with my mistrusting and manipulative behavior. But it was the first time I was willing to concede that the criticism was justified. And it was the first time I was willing to admit that my way of living life simply wasn't working. Life seemed far too difficult. I was far too unhappy. And I was making my friends and my family miserable, as well.

At that point, I felt as if I had no other choice but to do exactly what Randee suggested I do. Slowly—ever so slowly—I began to let go of my tenacious hold on how I thought things had to be.

And lo and behold, every time I let go, a miracle would occur.

The moment I let go of the idea that everything *had* to go my way, suddenly everything *did* go my way—maybe not the way I expected, but certainly in a way that was greatly to my benefit and to the benefit of all involved. Instead of working *against* me, it now felt as if the whole world was working *for* me. I experienced less stress, and more success. I let go. And I experienced the miracle of something called . . . the flow.

This book represents part of what I have learned over the last twenty-three years about what it means to let go and go with the flow. It is based on what I have personally experienced, and what I have come to believe after a long process of observation, contemplation, and what I consider to be nothing less than divine inspiration.

I am sharing these principles with you, dear reader, for one simple reason. They have helped me live a life that is immensely more joyful, dramatically more fulfilling, and, on top of it all, remarkably effortless. And I believe that if you follow these principles—principles that I have condensed into one easy-to-remember set of instructions—then you, too, can experience a life of greater happiness, satisfaction, and ease.

INTRODUCTION

Have you ever had a day in which everything seemed to go absolutely perfectly? A day in which you always seemed to be in the right place at the right time? A day that felt as if the entire universe was trying to make life easy for you? Would you like every day to be a day like that? Would you like every moment of every day to feel like one miracle happening after another? It's possible. It's called being in the flow. And that's what this book is about.

Being in the flow doesn't necessarily mean that your day will unfold exactly as you planned it, although that can happen. More often than not, it will mean experiencing something that's even better than what you planned, or at least its equivalent.

When you are in the flow, life ceases to be a struggle. You don't have to fight for what you want, or defend what you have. When you are in the flow your every need is met so easily, so completely, so consistently, there's only one reasonable explanation for it. There must be a higher power at work on your behalf.

It makes no difference whether you picture this higher power as a very real supreme being or some kind of conscious cosmic energy. The effect is the same. It feels as if something infinitely greater than yourself is operating in this world, and you are directly benefiting from its assistance.

I call this something God. But a more neutral term like Universal Intelligence, Divine Mind, Creator, or Source is equally valid if you are more comfortable with that. It is not my intention to impose a specific face on the source of this force that I call the flow. My intention is only to make you more aware of the flow's presence in your life, and to help you understand what you must do if you want to experience its miracles more freely and more frequently.

Fortunately, this is not a difficult thing to teach or to learn. For it is all summed up in this one short set of instructions:

ROW, ROW, ROW YOUR BOAT,
GENTLY DOWN THE STREAM,
MERRILY, MERRILY, MERRILY, MERRILY,
LIFE IS BUT A DREAM.

I'm sure you recognize these words as the lyrics to a simple little song you learned as a child. While most "rounds" of this kind came to us from England, this one is believed to have originated in the center of America—its author unknown—sometime in the mid-1800s. Perhaps oarsmen used this song to set the pace and relieve the tedium as they rowed up and down the Mississippi River.

Whatever its origins or actual intentions, I have found *Row, Row, Row Your Boat* to be a profound metaphor about how to live life more peacefully and abundantly. In a few short words, it tells you exactly how to get what you want out of life without stress or strain. It tells you how to manifest your fondest dreams almost effortlessly, and how to satisfy your deepest desires more fully.

Row, Row, Row Your Boat is a song about living life in the flow—the divine flow—and the sheer joy of the journey. Join me now as I explore this happy song word by word, and reveal its important message for us all.

I

YOUR BOAT

Every journey has a beginning. Yours began the day your boat was first launched into this world. And what a unique boat your boat is. No other boat looks exactly like yours. And no other boat navigates life in exactly the same way, because no other boat has been built with the same combination of talents, gifts, and abilities that yours has. To put it plainly, your boat is you. And you are a one-of-a-kind craft, unlike any other in all the universe.

Masterfully designed to move you through space and time, your body is the physical vessel itself. But no vessel goes anywhere undirected. There has to be someone on board who directs the body's travel and judges the journey's progress. That someone is your thinking mind.

Your mind is the decision maker—the brains of the boat, so to speak. It is the part of you that reasons, remembers, and reacts, interprets, analyzes, and chooses. But the mind is not the body's only passenger. Spirit is also on board.

Your spirit is the heart of your boat—its very life force and energy source. You may prefer to call your spirit your soul. Or you may choose to refer to it as your higher self, your true self, or even your God-self. By any name, your spirit is that eternal part of you that remains you, apart from the ever-changing body, and remains you, apart from the ever-changing mind. It is your divine essence. It is who you truly are at the core of your being, an individual expression of God, as inseparable from its origin as a wave is from the ocean.

These three—body, mind, and spirit—work together to help you glide gracefully through life. But a boat is not a boat just because it can float.

Any piece of driftwood can do that. A boat is a boat because it comes equipped with something that can take that boat in one particular direction or another. And in the case of a rowboat, that equipment is a set of oars.

Your oars are your free will. And your free will allows you to have a say-so in your own destiny. It gives you the freedom to decide where you want to go, what you want to do, what you want to have, and who you want to be. You can picture these desires as a lot of different destinations that you want to reach in life. Your free will enables you to row your boat toward any destination you wish. Your destination may be something you want to own, a relationship you want to nurture, a career you want to develop, or an adventure you want to experience. It might be as simple as a plan to meet someone for dinner. Or it might be as personal as a desire to heal a long-neglected emotional wound.

Some destinations may be close by and relatively quick to reach. Others, like your long-range goals and dreams, may lie farther away. Hopefully, you will eventually choose a destination that is directly related to the use of the talents, gifts, and abilities that are uniquely yours. Reaching that particular kind of destination will feel especially rewarding to you, because it may fulfill a mission that your spirit specifically came into this life to accomplish.

Whatever destination you choose—near or far, significant or frivolous—your free will empowers you to pursue it. But that doesn't mean that it's up to you, and you alone, to reach your dream. Because right there, just beneath your boat, lies the flow of a stream. And this stream is no ordinary stream. This stream has an intelligence all its own. It is ingeniously creative and immensely compassionate. And it is of equally loving service to every boat that floats upon it. This stream is nothing less than the divine flow of God's goodness. And it's there to help you get where you're going.

2

THE STREAM

The first time I consciously put my faith in the divine flow was on my way to work. That particular morning I had planned to exchange some crucial information with one of my co-workers. There was only one possible time we thought we could get together, and that was at 9:00 AM sharp. Not 8:55, because he would still be in a meeting. Not 9:05, because he was leaving to catch a plane. It was 9:00 or nothing.

Ordinarily that wouldn't have been a problem. But that day I was stuck in traffic on one of the city's most congested highways. I was faced with a choice. Should I just sit there and slowly inch my way to work, likely to miss my appointment? Or should I exit the highway and speed through the residential streets, twisting and turning and hoping to arrive in time? As a dyed-in-the-wool control freak, believe me, the second option seemed to be the best. At least there might be a slim chance that I could make it. But that day I chose differently. There are few more obvious flows in life than the flow of traffic. And that day something told me to go with the flow. I took a few deep breaths, popped in a soothing CD, and tried my best to patiently accept the slow but steady flow that finally delivered me to my office building . . . at 9:15.

I was fifteen minutes late. I had missed my appointment. I walked in the door and up to the elevator, wondering what I would do. You can imagine my surprise when the elevator door opened, and there stood my co-worker. His meeting had gone long, and now he was in more of a hurry than ever to get to the airport. But in that one short moment we had just enough time to conduct our important exchange.

Had I arrived at work one minute earlier I would have missed him. Had I arrived at work one minute later I would have missed him. But as it turned out, it was perfect. I went with the flow, and the flow put me in exactly the right place at exactly the right time.

I know, as miracles go, this is a fairly minor one to tell you about. But I chose this story, and all the stories to follow, for a very specific reason. Most of life is not about huge, life-changing miracles. It's just about getting through each day as pleasantly, as peacefully, and as prosperously as possible. When you go with the divine flow, yes, you will experience major miracles—life-changing miracles even. But you will also experience lots of little ones—each and every day—making every moment of your life a joy to be lived. And to me, that is what *Row, Row, Row Your Boat* is really all about.

Row, Row, Row Your Boat is based on the single premise that there is, indeed, an underlying current in your life—a steadily flowing stream—

that is continually guiding you toward the fulfillment of your heart's desires in the most beneficial way possible.

Sometimes this stream is obvious, like the flow of traffic I just described. Other times the stream is subtler, occurring as a series of coincidences and synchronicities that you might miss if you're not paying attention.

The stream may feel extremely supportive, by offering you a golden opportunity through an unexpected phone call or an unplanned encounter. Or, you may run into a situation that feels disastrous—like getting laid off from work—and have to trust that this, too, is the stream, giving you a chance to take your life in a new and better direction.

Even the speed of the stream may vary. It may move quickly, swiftly leading you to your good. Or it may feel as if it is hardly moving at all, leaving you in still waters for days on end with no clear guidance or direction. This may be the stream telling you to wait patiently because divine timing is at work.

In more traditional terms, this stream—this ever-present and everywhere-present divine flow—could be described as God's will at work in your life. But let me be clear about how I see God's will.

I see God's will for you as what God *wants* for you. That is my way of saying that God's will for you is not a command. It is not something that God specifically dictates or mandates, leaving you little or no choice in the matter . . . quite the opposite. As I said in chapter 1, I believe that God gives you the freedom to choose whatever it is you want out of life. Then, in response, God supports you in fulfilling that desire.

It's like the relationship between a truly loving parent and his or her beloved child. All God really wants is for you to be happy and to enjoy life. Do you want to slide down the slide? Then God will help you climb to the top. Do you want to swing on the swings? Then God will give you a push. Does the thought of becoming a doctor, a teacher, a writer, or a carpenter bring you joy? Then God will help you find the money to fund your training, and help you make the necessary contacts to establish your career.

As with any truly loving parent, it is God's great pleasure to help you in every conceivable (and inconceivable) way to realize your dream. But, like any truly loving parent, God also keeps your best interests in mind, knowing that you may have a somewhat limited view of what is actually good for you. That means that God will help you get to your good, yes, but God will always make sure that it's your *highest* good. What exactly do I mean by highest good?

First of all, your highest good is good! And I don't mean good in the sense of, "This is going to hurt, but it's good for you." Personally, I don't believe that God ever intends for you to suffer. Not at any time. Not in any way. What loving parent ever wants his or her child to be in pain? No, I believe that your highest good is *all* good, and *nothing but* good.

Second, your highest good is good for all. Your good can never come at the expense of another's. God loves everyone equally. So God will take what you want and make it work out in a way that benefits everybody, which is something that is often too complex for you to imagine, let alone for you to orchestrate on your own. But all things are possible with God. That's what makes God . . . well . . . God.

Third, your highest good is unlimited good. Ask yourself this. When you decide upon a destination, do you always make it the greatest and grandest destination that you could ever hope to reach? Not likely. Identifying more with your human nature than your spiritual nature, you forget whose child you really are, and how generous your true parent really is. You limit yourself, not daring to ask for too much for fear of your request being denied. Even if you do allow yourself an occasional flight of fancy—conjuring up an immensely satisfying scenario for yourself—you soon abandon the idea as an impossible dream.

But again, all things are possible with God. In God's mind there are no limits to where you can go, what you can have, what you can do, and who you can be. What God knows is possible for you is always far grander than what you think is possible for yourself. The only limitations in life are the ones that you yourself put on it.

Finally, your highest good is an *experience* of good. Sure, there may be some material things that you desire in particular, but most of the material things you want in life are actually just symbols for an experience you want to have—an experience of comfort, abundance, security, peace, freedom, and so on. Your highest good will always give you the experience that you are seeking. But it won't necessarily manifest as the *specific thing* you've chosen to stand for that experience.

For instance, you may want a new car because the one you currently own is costing you a fortune in unexpected repair bills. But what you really desire is an experience of financial stability and reliable mobility. Your highest good, then, might turn out to be a better-paying job that just happens to be within walking distance of your home! And who knows, with the extra money you earn in your new job, plus the extra money you save by walking, you may one day end up buying a new car after all . . . only now it may be a car that you could never have afforded before!

When it comes to satisfying your heart's desires, the stream of God's goodness is infinite in its inventiveness. And you can always depend on it to help deliver you to your destination with miraculous ease. That doesn't mean, however, that the stream is simply going to pick you up, carry you along, and drop you off there.

The divine flow leads. It guides. It directs. It supports. But it doesn't live your life for you. The gift of free will requires its use. To get where you want to go, you're going to have to pick up your oars and row.

3

ROW, ROW, ROW

To row, row, row is to use your free will to move you closer, closer, and closer still to your chosen destination. As I have said, the sole aim of the flow is to help deliver you to your heart's desire in the most beneficial way possible. But you will never just magically appear at the journey's end. Getting there is a step-by-step process, and your free will is involved every step of the way.

Through synchronistic events and happy coincidences, the flow will open doors for you and create opportunities for you in direct response to your desire. But you must choose, of your own free will, to go through those doors and take advantage of those opportunities. There will always be some kind of choice you must make, and some kind of action you must take to move you forward. Even if God were to hand you a gift on a silver platter, you would still have to decide to reach out and take it. That's a choice of free will. That's an act of free will. That's rowing. And you are free to row with the flow . . . or not. It's totally up to you.

If the divine flow is God's will at work in your life, then once again you can see how God supports you in the same way that a truly loving parent supports his or her child. As long as what you want does not diminish anyone else's good— and is not damaging to yourself—then God will provide you with all the assistance you need to go where you want to go, do what you want to do, have what you want to have, and be what you want to be. You will have to do the footwork. But God will pave the way for you, showing you the next right step to take.

By "next right step" I don't mean to imply

that there is ever really a *wrong* step. I will explain in chapter 5 how you can row in almost any direction and still reach your highest good. I do believe, however, that from where you are at any given moment, there is one step that you can take that will be the most effective and efficient way of reaching your destination. That's the next right step. And invariably it will be a step that is right in front of you and relatively easy to do.

I say *relatively* easy, because occasionally the next right step may require you to step a little out of your personal comfort zone. But generally, the next right step will not be anything that you or anyone else would ever consider to be overly difficult. I had just that kind of step presented to me soon after I began working on the manuscript for this book.

Even though my desire was to eventually have this manuscript published, I continually avoided looking into the publishing process because I was afraid of being overwhelmed by what it might entail. I thought I might get so discouraged by what I found out that I would stop writing this book altogether.

One day, my lovely partner, Carol, mentioned that I might want to call FUN/ED, the local adult education center, to see if they had a class on publishing. But I ignored her suggestion, preferring to keep my head buried in the sand. "How likely would it be for FUN/ED to have a class on publishing, anyway?" I asked myself. "Not very," I decided.

Then one Sunday I was at lunch with a group of friends from church, and I overheard my friend, Larry, telling another one of my friends that he had just signed up to take an evening class at FUN/ED. Hmmm. There it was again . . . FUN/ED. At that moment, I got the feeling that it was important for me to break into their conversation, and ask Larry what the class he was going to take was all about. So I did. And his reply? "How to Publish a Non-Fiction Book."

I knew without a doubt that this was the flow presenting the next right step to me, and it would be foolish of me to ignore its guidance again. When Larry told me how easy it was to sign up for FUN/ED classes over the Internet, I suddenly remembered that for the last month I had been driving by a billboard displaying FUN/ED's Internet address. Could I have been given a clearer sign?

That night I accessed FUN/ED's Web site and enrolled in not one, but two classes. And guess what? Instead of being overwhelmed or discouraged by what I learned, I came away from those classes with the confidence and peace of mind that I could, indeed, handle the publishing process. And more than that, I gained an important personal contact in the publishing industry. I met the person who turned out to be the publisher of this very book!

It sounds so simple, doesn't it? There's somewhere that you want to go, and the divine flow tells you exactly where to row. But if this is true, why don't you experience the flow more often than you do? Well, it's for the same reason I did not immediately recognize that my next right step was to call FUN/ED. There are numerous barriers that can restrict your ability to take full and frequent advantage of the divine flow. If you want to avoid those barriers, you must be able to answer yes to the following five questions:

Question #1
"Do you really want to go where you say you do?"

Often, what you say you want and what you say is true is contradicted by what you really think and what you really feel, deep down inside. I said I wanted to publish this book. But I was so intimidated by the publishing process itself, I actively resisted the flow's very first attempt to lead me to the one place that could quickly and easily remove my fears and make publishing a probability instead of a problem.

If you want to avoid this kind of self-sabotage, try to be as honest with yourself as you can be about your desire. Make sure that all your thoughts and feelings about it are in complete agreement. If they are, then let God know what your desire is in no uncertain terms. In your mind's eye, picture your desire as already fulfilled. But don't just *see* it, *experience* it! Use all of your senses to imagine what it would be like to have your dream come true. What do your ears hear? What do your hands touch? What does your nose smell? What does your tongue taste? Make your visualization as vivid as possible—a pleasant daydream that you return to time and time again.

The last two homes I purchased came miraculously into my possession through just such a process of vivid visualization. In both cases, even though it seemed highly unlikely that either of those two homes could be mine, I continued to daydream about things like mowing the lawn, building more cabinets, and taking my children to trick-or-treat up and down the street on Halloween. In my mind, I was already living there. And the next thing I knew, I actually was.

Don't underestimate the power of your imagination. One clear-cut intention on your part is enough to set the entire flow in motion, initiating a complex series of cosmic events that occur solely to help you reach your destination successfully.

Above all, remember that you are worthy of having whatever it is that you desire. One of the most common forms of self-sabotage is a hidden, underlying feeling that you don't deserve to have your dream come true, because you are not good enough to have it or capable enough to handle it. Nonsense. As a holy and wholly loved child of God, whatever you desire is already yours by divine right. But you must be willing to accept your inheritance. Claim it now!

QUESTION #2
"Are you paying attention
to what's going on around you?"

One of my all-time favorite sayings is, "There's God, and There's Not Paying Attention." That means there is never a time when God is not trying to point you in the direction of your greatest good. God is always—and in all ways—showing you the next right step to take. God communicates with you through books, magazines, newspapers, poetry, Scripture, and sermons; through movies, TV shows, radio programs, and the Internet; even through nature. But of all the ways that God communicates with you, one of the most common is through the people who are put in your path—through your family and friends, your co-workers and acquaintances, your ministers, teachers, therapists, and even total strangers. In order to get the message, however, *you have to pay attention!*

I drove by that FUN/ED billboard every single day for an entire month. But all I did was *look* at it. I didn't really *see* it. Lost in my own thoughts, I left no room in my mind for the flow's guidance to register. And what was I thinking about so hard, anyway? I guarantee you it was one of only two possible things:

something in the past or something in the future—both of which block all awareness of the flow.

To be able to row with the flow, you must be fully present in the current moment. When you are replaying the past in your head or projecting a possible future in your mind, you cannot fully experience what's going on right here and right now. And right here and right now is where the flow happens. Here is where the opportunities are. Here is where the guidance is. Here is where God lives and speaks to you. Be here. Now.

QUESTION #3
"Are you paying attention
to what's going on within you?"

When I was at lunch with my friends from church, I got a funny feeling the second I heard Larry mention FUN/ED. It was like an internal alarm clock going off inside my body. Even though I was still resisting the idea of FUN/ED, at that moment something told me—no, compelled me—to get involved in the conversation. That something was my very own spirit. I had already ignored two of the flow's outer messengers—Carol and the billboard—and now my own inner messenger, my spirit, was trying to make sure I didn't miss what Larry had to say.

Your spirit is the single most valuable and reliable source of guidance you have. As an individual expression of God, it is your direct, personal link to divine wisdom. You can always trust your spirit to know what the next right step should be. And your spirit is always attempting to tell you what that step is, or at least make you aware of it.

Commonly called intuition, your spirit may communicate with you through a thought, an image, a dream, or that still, small voice inside your head. Or, if your mind is too preoccupied, your spirit may try to reach you through your body, with the kind of sudden sensation that is sometimes called a gut feeling.

If your gut feeling is fear, try to determine if there is a genuine, impending threat to your bodily safety. If you do not appear to be in immediate physical danger, but you remain fearful, there may be an issue from your own personal history that needs to be addressed. Your apprehension could be related to a painful experience from your past that is no longer relevant. Or, your anxiety may be due to a belief that is, in truth, unfounded— an idea that you are being abandoned, for example. Often this kind of fear can be so acute, you may sense that your very survival is at stake. But that sensation is not your spirit speaking. And it is wise to avoid basing a decision on that kind of unreasonable fear—*especially* if your decision will deprive someone else of his or her good.

Keep in mind that your spirit is your God-self. So, as a general rule, your spirit will speak to you only in a way that is God-like—through messages that are beneficial and life-affirming for all, and through feelings that are positive, uplifting, and enlivening. If a step you decide to take comes from a place of peace, that is a very good indication that your decision is based on the wisdom of your spirit. If a goal you decide to set is accompanied by bliss, that is most likely your spirit blessing your choice and telling you, "Yes! This is what you are here to do!" Whenever you feel exceptionally energized by an endeavor that you are engaged in—especially one that causes you to lose all track of time—you can bet that your spirit is the source of your endless energy.

It is no coincidence that one of the most common words used to describe these various kinds of encouraging feelings is enthusiasm, which is derived from the Greek word *entheos*—"God within!" So whenever you feel enthusiastic about something, by all means follow your bliss. Go for it! Row for it! You have been inspired by your spirit—the spirit of God within you.

And don't forget, you don't have to wait for your spirit to get in touch with you. Anytime you feel a need for divine guidance, you can get quiet, go within, and request the counsel of your higher self. There is no better way to follow the flow than to constantly stop and seek direction through prayer and meditation.

QUESTION #4
"Are you willing to let go of what you think you know?"

Few among us have been trained to trust anyone or anything other than our own self-serving egos. Believing in signs may seem fool-hardy to you. Paying attention to your intuition, fanciful. And putting your faith in some unseen force called the flow? Come on. It's a nice idea, but a bit naïve, isn't it?

If you are like most people, chances are you have been raised to be fairly self-reliant. There's only one problem with that. The self that you are relying on is unreliable. Why? Because what you experience as your *self* is primarily your *mind*. And your mind is full of "facts" that are little more than false assumptions and half-truths that are based on information that is incomplete at best. I will talk more about this in chapter 6, but suffice it to say that when compared to the wisdom of your *true* self—your spirit—what your mind thinks it knows is extremely limited and highly biased.

So, even though your mind is ultimately responsible for deciding what the next right step is, that decision should never be based solely on your mind's own storehouse of supposed knowledge. You must take your intuition as seriously as your intellect, and respect its guidance as much as you respect logic, reason, and all that misinformation in your mind that you value as "what you know." Otherwise, your ability to row with the flow will be seriously inhibited. How, exactly?

Well, for one thing, the more you think you know, the more likely you are to completely miss or dismiss the next right step because, from your limited point of view, it just doesn't look reasonable to you. A perfect example is the time I needed to buy a sleeping bag for a campout.

One evening, a few weeks before my trip, I decided to eat at one of my favorite Italian restaurants. I was surprised when I pulled up to the building to see that they were closed, so I drove down the street to another Italian restaurant instead. As I sat at my table and looked out the window, I noticed that there was a sporting goods store just across the parking lot. "Perfect," I thought. "The flow has delivered me right to the doorstep of the best place to buy a sleeping bag!"

But then logic crept in. I remembered that this particular sporting goods store was one of the most expensive ones in town. Even if they were having a sale, I "knew" that their sale price would be more than the regular price at a discount store. So, after dinner, instead of simply walking across the parking lot to take a look, I drove to a discount store a good five miles away.

I got my sleeping bag. And I got it for what

I thought was a reasonable price, too. But the next morning, a friend of mine showed me an advertisement in the previous day's newspaper. It was an ad for the sporting goods store that was next door to the restaurant where I had eaten. Apparently I had, indeed, missed a sale—a One-Day-Only Super Sale. And one of the featured items in the ad? A sleeping bag that was twice as nice, for half the price that I had paid. I had let reason interfere with the flow, and it cost me.

A much-more-costly consequence can occur when what you think you know prevents you from reaching your destination altogether. This often happens when you look beyond the next right step to all the additional steps you think will be required. Thinking ahead like that can be extremely debilitating in several different ways.

You may look ahead at all the steps you believe you will have to take, and all the decisions you believe you will have to make, and feel so overwhelmed by what

you imagine, you may quit the journey
before you even begin it.

Or, you may remain frozen in fear because
you *don't* know what all the steps required
may be, but you think you *should* know, and
you won't act until you *do* know.

Or, you may set out toward your goal,
but when things don't go the way you
think they should, you may believe that
your goal is unreachable, so you give up.
You may tell yourself things such as "I
don't have what it takes to get it," or
"God doesn't want me to have it."

In some cases, even looking just *one* step
beyond the next right step can be counterproduc-
tive. A few years ago, Carol, who used to lease
apartments for a living, had the opportunity to
interview for a leasing position at a brand-new,
loft-type complex—a complex built by the same
company that owned and operated the property
where she had been working for thirteen years.
Her friends and I thought it would be an excellent

move for her, and that it was God's answer to her growing desire to work in a more desirable area of the city.

But Carol kept dragging her feet. Day after day, she kept putting off making the call to set up an interview. Something about working at the lofts didn't feel like a perfect fit to her, and she couldn't decide whether she should interview for the job or not.

Nevertheless, growing increasingly unhappy with her current situation, she finally decided to go ahead and interview for the position—in spite of her reservations. Although Carol was one of the most highly respected and successful leasing agents in the entire company, in the end, she wasn't offered the job. However, once the word was out that Carol was willing to work at a community other than the one where she appeared to be so firmly entrenched, she immediately received an offer to work at another community—a community that had actually been her true heart's desire all along!

Do you see the point here? It's a little subtle, so allow me to spell it out. Carol's misgivings about the interview had absolutely nothing to do with taking the next right step. She was one step ahead of herself, agonizing about whether or not she would enjoy working at the lofts. But she hadn't even been offered the job! The next right step was simply to go to the interview. That's all. Just go to the interview. The interview did not necessarily mean that she would be offered the job. And it did not mean that she would have to accept the position even if it were offered. The interview was simply the flow's way of opening up a route that would help deliver Carol to her dream. Had Carol not overcome her resistance to interviewing (thanks, in part, to a little encouragement from her friends), she might have missed this ideal opportunity, or delayed its manifestation in her life.

Listen up. Knowing what lies down the stream is not your job. Your job is only to decide where you want to go, and then take each right step as it comes along, *remaining focused solely on that single step.*

It is impossible for you to predict what all the next right steps will be, anyway, because they change with every choice you make and every stroke you take. The flow has no alternative but to present one right step to you at a time, because the next right step after that one may be completely different, based on the effects of your freewill decision.

If you want your journey to be a peaceful and effortless experience, you must be willing to let go of what you think you know, and allow a greater mind—the unlimited, creative intelligence of the flow—to orchestrate the details.

QUESTION #5
"Do you know what 'effortless'
even feels like?"

Rowing with the flow is virtually effortless. But you will never know if you are in the flow if you don't have a very good feel for what effort-lessness is. Were you told as a child that life is supposed to be easy? Or were you told that life is inescapably hard? Were you told that the universe is at your service, ready to fulfill your every heart's desire? Or were you told that you have to struggle for what you want, and fight to hold on to what you have?

If you were brought up to believe that life is difficult because it's *supposed* to be difficult— that it may even be God's way of testing you—then you may have developed a very high tolerance for pain. Stress may be something that you are so accustomed to feeling, you may not even realize that you are experiencing it.

If a continual level of anxiety and tension is normal for you—even if it's a fairly low level—you will have a hard time recognizing the flow and its telltale traits of ease and effortlessness. Almost any step that occurs to you may seem like the next right step, as long as it appears to lead to your goal. How easy it is may be irrelevant to you. In fact, you may even feel a fair amount of pride about your ability to persevere in the face of seemingly insurmountable odds. And Western society will applaud you for that.

There's an old adage in this culture that says, "When the going gets tough, the tough get going."* You are told that with enough willpower you can make almost anything happen. And you know what? You can. With enough determination you can row, row, row—oblivious to the flow—until you reach almost any destination you set out for. But have you ever worked really hard to fulfill a desire and, once you did, felt strangely unsatisfied by it? Have you ever struggled to achieve something and, in the end, realized that you had injured others along the way? Has there ever been anything that you really wanted, pushed hard to get, and, when all was said and done, actually regretted getting?

Perhaps you rowed too hard and for too long.

You got what you wanted, but maybe not what you needed . . . and not what was best for all. Perhaps you should have rowed more gently.

---

* Although many popular sayings have an unknown origin, this one is commonly attributed to U.S. tycoon and diplomat, Joseph P. Kennedy. It has also been ascribed to legendary football coach, Knute Rockne.

4

GENTLY

To row gently simply means to remain flexible to the flow, and to refrain from forcing things to go the way you think they should. Now don't get me wrong. I'm not suggesting that you never plan ahead. A plan is nothing more than a combination of desires—generally, a desire of where you want to go, coupled with a desire of how you want to get there. And there's nothing wrong with desires. As I said earlier in this book, your desires set the whole flow in motion in the first place.

So go ahead and plan all you want. Plan your day. Plan your week. Plan your whole year if you want to. Just don't become overly attached to those plans. To row with the flow you must be willing to abandon your preconceived ideas about how things should progress. Again, rowing a boat is an excellent metaphor for this concept, because most classic rowboats are designed for you, the rower, to sit facing backwards. That means that you have a pretty good idea about where you're headed, but you're not continually fixated on it.

When you remain rigidly attached to a plan—following your predetermined course come heck or high water—you have gone beyond taking the next right step and have moved into the willful world of manipulation and control. You are no longer taking advantage of the flow's effortless opportunities. Instead, you are literally forcing your way forward, relying solely on the strength of your own will to influence people and orchestrate events to get where you want to go. You are on your own. And as a result, you are much more likely to encounter obstacles the flow would have naturally steered you clear of.

To row gently, you must remain sensitive to

the flow as you row, pausing after each and every stroke to determine whether you are still rowing in the same direction that the current is flowing. It commonly works like this:

You pick what you believe to be a worthwhile destination—a new car, a bigger house, a better job—and you start rowing toward it. You row, row, row, taking each right step as it comes along to acquire that car, that house, that job. If what you want seems to fall right into your lap, good for you! You were in the flow the entire way, and the flow—as promised—effortlessly guided you to your goal.

What usually happens, however, is that the going gets a little rough at some point. People aren't cooperating. The timing isn't working out. Roadblocks keep arising. You find that you have to exert more and more effort to move ahead. You begin to feel tense and anxious. Heed those feelings and notice those signs, for those are the signals that the flow may be going in one direction, while you are rowing in another.

It's at this point in the stream that you have an important decision to make. Do you push on, continuing to row in the same direction you were rowing? Do you pay yet another visit to the automobile dealership? Do you make yet another phone call to the mortgage company? Do you send yet another letter to the prospective employer? Or, instead, do you take your oars out of the water, and for a moment—just for a moment—do nothing at all?

Society might say, "Forge on! You can do it! You can make it happen!" And as I said before, you can. The force of your will is that strong. But is it better to *make* something happen, or *let* something happen?

The central teaching of *Row, Row, Row Your Boat* is that when the going gets tough, the *tough* may get going, but the *wise* stop rowing. This may sound like giving up. But you are not giving up. You are opening up. You are attuning yourself to the feel of the flow, so you can continue to follow its guidance and once again glide toward your goal with effortless ease.

There is no big mystery or magic surrounding attunement. Attuning yourself to the feel of the flow is just another way of saying what we have all been advised to do at an unprotected railroad crossing. Stop. Look. And listen. Stop what you're doing. Look around you for any signs that might tell you which way you should point your boat. And above all, listen to what your spirit has to say. Try to find a quiet place where you can hear that still, small voice. If at all possible, take time to pray, meditate, or journal about where you are, and where you'd prefer to be.

When you let go of what you think you know and attune yourself to the feel of the flow, you will be more able to clearly discern what the next right step should be. And when you take that step—when you choose to once again row *with* the flow and not *against* it—it will feel as if the entire universe is supporting you in your new direction. Because it is.

One memorable experience with attunement

occurred when Karen, a mutual friend of Carol's and mine, gave me a free pass to a movie. The movie was playing at a theater in a shopping complex that I had never been to before. Our only plan was to meet at the theater around 7:00 PM.

I decided that I would arrive early, explore the complex, and then have dinner in one of the restaurants before the show. Returning the favor of the free pass, I called Karen to see if she wanted to join me for the meal, but she wasn't home. So I left a message on her answering machine to meet me at a particular restaurant at 6:00 . . . that is, if she was able to. The restaurant I chose was not a particularly good one, but it was the only one I knew about.

When I arrived at the complex, I quickly discovered a much better restaurant than the one I had suggested. With no good way to reach Karen, I felt that I had no choice but to stick to the plan. So I continued to look around the various shops until I finally ended up at the original restaurant I had recommended. It was crowded. It was noisy.

And I was thirty minutes early.

I no longer felt like I was in the flow. I didn't like where I was, and I didn't relish the idea of waiting there for half an hour—especially since I didn't even know if Karen would be coming or not. I began to feel very uncomfortable. I didn't know what to do. All I knew was that it was so noisy in there I could hardly hear myself think. And then something deep within me urged me to "go outside." What? "Go outside." Why? "Just go outside." It was my spirit speaking.

I followed my spirit's advice and stepped out the door. Ahhh . . . the peace, the quiet. Now I could hear my spirit more clearly than ever. "Go to the other restaurant." Are you sure? "Go to the other restaurant." What happens if Karen shows up at 6:00 looking for me? "Go to the other restaurant."

Once again, I followed my inner guidance, trying my best to put my faith in the flow and rely on its direction. Perhaps I will run into Karen along the way, I thought. That would definitely

be in the flow. Or once I'm in the restaurant,
maybe I'll see her pass by the window. That
would certainly be convenient. Worst-case scenario, if I've totally misjudged the flow, when
6:00 rolls around I'll run back to the first restaurant and see if Karen's there.

Have you figured out the end of the story
yet? I'm sure you have. I arrived at the new
restaurant, settled in at a table, ordered some tea,
then looked across the room to see . . . yes . . . you
guessed it . . . Karen. She was standing next to
a display table looking over an array of recommended wines. As it turned out, this particular
restaurant was one of Karen's favorites. And
since she knew it had both a front and a rear
entrance, she often used it as a cut-through on her
way from the parking garage to the shops.

It was now 6:00 on the dot, and Karen and I
were about to enjoy a magnificent dinner, in
addition to a marvelous movie. Similar to the
time I was stuck in traffic on my way to the
office, I let go, I followed the flow, and the flow

put me in exactly the right place at exactly the right time. Perfect. Just perfect.

Again, this story is no major miracle—not by a long shot. But it does illustrate a few of the things you need to know if you want to row gently with the flow.

FIRST,
You can't avoid turbulence
if you don't realize you're in it.
Learn how to recognize
when the rowing is getting rough.
Do you feel tense? Anxious? Confused?
Are doors closing? Is the timing off?
Pay attention to that.

SECOND,
You can't feel the flow
if you're still stirring up the stream.
Take your oars out of the water
and quit rowing for a moment.
Stop doing. Begin being.

THIRD,
It's hard to see the signs or hear the messages
if you've rowed into chaos.
Find a quiet place where you can be
more receptive to guidance.
The best quiet place is within yourself,
which happens to be
where the best guidance is, as well.

FOURTH,
You can't row with the flow if you're
unwilling to make frequent course corrections.
Become as fluid as the flow.
Row. Attune yourself to the flow. Row.
Attune yourself to the flow.
Be willing to continually adjust
to the course of the current.

Are you willing to gently follow the flow
wherever it may go? Are you willing—as they
say—to "Let Go and Let God?" I still remember
the first time I ever heard that saying. I didn't

have the faintest idea of what it meant. It didn't even seem to be a complete sentence to me. Let go? Let go of *what?* I wasn't holding onto anything, I thought. And let God? Let God *what?* Let God *do* something? What does God really *do?*

It wasn't that I didn't believe in God at that time. I had no doubt that some kind of God existed—some kind of divine power—and that this God was responsible for setting the whole world in motion. I just wasn't sure how involved God was after that. Nothing in my conscious awareness had ever indicated to me that God was, or even could be, an active force in my life.

So—not expecting God's help, not looking for God's help—I continued to will my way through life, depending only on the force of my own personal power to move ahead. I rowed and I rowed and I rowed and I rowed, until eventually, the going got so rough, and life got so tough, I was forced to admit that perhaps my way was not the best way after all. For once in my life, I became willing to relinquish my control. And that little opening was all God needed to get through to me, and for me to begin to see that God was, indeed, present and active in my life.

Traditionally, this idea of relinquishing control—of letting go and letting God do what only God can do—has been called surrender. But sometimes the word surrender is confused with resignation. You let go, but you do it begrudgingly. Deep down inside you still harbor the idea that you know best. You can't fight God, though, can you? So you give up—you throw up the white flag and surrender—resigning yourself to whatever God wills for you . . . only you're not so sure you're going to like what God's will is.

Know this. Letting go and letting God is not about resignation. And it is not a convenient excuse for just sitting around and waiting for God to hand you a life, either. It is still up to you to decide what you want to get out of life. And it is still up to you to live that life, by taking the actions you need to take, as the flow guides you toward your chosen goal. As Frank, the minister at my former church, once put it, "Without an objective there is no journey. There is only drifting." And letting go and letting God is definitely not about drifting.

Letting go and letting God is about trusting—trusting that the divine flow will always guide you to your desired good. Always. But to trust the flow, you have to let go of your *specific* ideas about how you're going to get to that good. And more than that, to trust the flow you have to let go of your *specific* ideas about what that good is.

It may be that car you wanted. Or, it may be something else that gives you the freedom that car represents to you. It may be that house you wanted. Or, it may be something else that gives you the security that house represents to you. It may be that job you wanted. Or, it may be something else that gives you the abundance that job represents to you.

No matter what it is that you are specifically rowing toward, God knows what you really need.

And to row gently is to allow God to lead you to what you *need* instead of what you *want*. It is to be willing to let God guide you in a direction that is different from the one you originally planned on, knowing that it will always lead to your *highest* good—to your *greatest* joy and to the *best* outcome for all concerned. That is why I recommend that whenever you pray for the fulfillment of any specific desire, you remain open to your highest good by including this statement in your prayer: "I desire this, its equivalent, or something greater. Thank you, God."

And if you don't? If you don't stay open? If you don't row gently? If you continue to row against the flow because you still think that you know best? Don't worry. Your highest good is still ahead of you. It will just be a little farther down the stream—or *up* the stream, if that's the direction you're headed.

5

DOWN

A friend of mine, who goes by Rusty, has a favorite expression. He often says, "Why go north to get south?" He is referring to the fact that the world is round, and yes, it is physically possible to get to a place that lies *down* the stream by heading *up* the stream. You can, if you so choose, encircle the entire globe and eventually arrive at your chosen destination. But what an unnecessarily arduous journey that would be!

Nevertheless, when you inadvertently ignore the flow or willfully resist it, you may be doing just that. You are rowing upstream to get downstream. You are going the long way around. And that way can be extremely difficult. Without the benefit of the flow helping you get where you want to go, your every effort to move forward will be just that . . . an effort. What's more, as I have previously pointed out, you are much more likely to run into a few unexpected obstacles as a direct or indirect result of your unguided choices and your misguided actions.

The beauty of the divine flow, though, is that it never leaves you stuck on a sandbar or spinning in a whirlpool because you rowed along a route that, in hindsight, you would not choose again. Even if you wind up halfway around the world, you are not—as it is commonly put—up the creek without a paddle.

No matter what kind of directional error you think you might have made, the flow is always right there, awaiting only the return of your awareness of it and your willingness to follow it once again. No matter what kind of undesirable situation you think you may have rowed yourself into, the flow is always ready to guide you to your highest good *from right where you are.*

Often, the opportunity that appears will arise so naturally and so perfectly out of your current situation, it may look as if you had to go through whatever it is you went through to get to your highest good. But did you?

Contrary to what some may say about God's will, I do not believe that the difficult circumstances you encounter in life are part of some kind of divine plan to help you grow in character. I'm not saying that these experiences can't help you learn some valuable emotional and spiritual lessons. They can. Challenges always provide you with a tremendous opportunity to develop qualities like courage, compassion, understanding, and so on. And that's wonderful. I'm just saying that these challenging events are not in your life *specifically by divine design.*

As I said in chapter 2, I don't believe that God ever intends for you to suffer. That means that God does not purposefully put obstacles in your path, or lead you along a route that is unnecessarily circuitous. God doesn't have to create

a challenging journey for you, because you set
yourself up for one every time you row against
the flow. Challenges are to be expected in life,
because they are the natural result of making
any freewill choice that causes you to veer off
your divinely directed course. And that's true
no matter how innocent or well-meaning your
choice may have been. Remember, too, that there
are countless other freewill choices being made in
this world, and even with the best of intentions—
or simply because of inattention—you can easily
make yourself vulnerable to the consequences of
those decisions.

The good news is—no, the *great* news is—
God, being infinitely creative, can take any decision that you make, or any decision that anyone
else makes, and transform it into an ideal
opportunity for all involved to reach their highest
good. This is something that I grow increasingly
grateful for each and every day. For as a child,
I decided that once a mistake was made, there
was no recovery from it. The effect of every

misstep would be everlasting and could never be undone. No wonder I grew up to be such a perfectionist. One slip-up and I thought I was doomed for all time!

My actual experience, however, has proved to me that with the divine flow there is no such thing as "You can't get there from here." The gracious guidance of the flow never ceases, and it is always available wherever you are. When I resisted Carol's suggestion to call FUN/ED about publishing classes, for instance, the flow gave me a billboard with the FUN/ED Internet address on it. When I ignored the billboard, the flow gave me Larry, who had just signed up for one of FUN/ED's publishing classes. I don't know if the flow would have continued indefinitely to guide me toward FUN/ED, but I *am* convinced that it would have continued indefinitely to offer me the easiest possible path to publishing, from right where I was.

Remember, learning how to row with the flow is like learning any other skill. It takes practice, and it takes patience. Just do the best you can.

Before you begin your journey, ask yourself a few questions. Is there anything about your chosen destination that would obviously harm another? No? Good. Do you feel energized and enthusiastic about your destination? Yes? Great. Do you think you know what the next right step is? You do? Terrific! Then take that step. But if the going gets rough—if it turns out that your destination was *not* for the good of all, that your energy was more about ego than enthusiasm, and that you were actually rowing against the flow and you don't like where you ended up—don't lose heart.

If you ever find yourself somewhere that you'd rather not be, know that there is always a door leading directly to your desire that is right there and ready to swing open the moment you are willing to see it. But also know that, to see it, you must be willing to suspend your judgment about where you are. You must be willing to look at things differently—more distantly—as if life were but a dream. Because in a way, that's exactly what life is.

6

A Dream

To say that life is but a dream is to say that what you consider to be reality may seem very real to you, but it may not seem as real to anyone else. This is because you instantly give meaning to every single circumstance that occurs in your life. You judge it and label it as good, bad, or indifferent. But the meaning you give to these circumstances is greatly influenced by your own personal history and belief system. Another person looking at the same situation may see an entirely different picture, based on his or her own unique past. Like a dream, then, each person sees what he or she chooses to see, and interprets his or her vision the way he or she chooses to interpret it.

This phenomenon of subjective reality is called perception. Perception is not the same as True Knowing. True Knowing comes directly from your spirit. It is a deeply felt and unshifting sense of surety. Perception, on the other hand, is highly relative and easily subject to change. When viewed from another angle or a different perspective, what you once perceived to be true can alter significantly.

Since you can never really know everything there is to know about any given situation, and since everything you perceive is colored in some way by your interpretation of it, then all perception is to some degree a *misperception*. If you use your perception to hastily label an occurrence as bad, and then rashly act on that combination of misinformation and misinterpretation, you may miss the very opportunity that could lead you to your highest good. Here is an example.

In the fall of 2001, Carol and I decided to drive from Dallas, Texas, to St. Louis, Missouri, to visit her mother. To make the long journey more pleasurable, we decided to split the trip into three parts. Our plan was to drive to Hot Springs, Arkansas, on the first day. We would spend the second day digging for quartz crystals in one of their public open-pit mines. And on the third day we would continue on to St. Louis, arriving in time, hopefully, to eat at a quaint riverside restaurant located in a historic settlement just south of the city.

After spending the night in Hot Springs, we arose early the next morning to a light mist. Hmmm . . . rain certainly wasn't in the plan. What now? You can't dig for crystals in the rain. But still, it was early in the day and it was just a light mist. Perhaps it would clear up, we thought. So we listened to our intuition and took what we believed to be the next right step. We went out for breakfast.

Before the coffee was poured the mist had turned into a monsoon. It certainly looked as if the flow had other plans for us. So after breakfast, we took what we believed to be the next right step. We went back to the hotel, packed our bags, and checked out. By this time the rain had stopped. But thinking that it would now be too muddy to dig, we got into the car and began to drive out of town.

About two miles down the road, we approached a crystal shop whose owner we had met on an earlier visit to Hot Springs. We were about to pass by the shop when something told us (our intuition again) to stop and look in the shop's window. We did. And even though it was only 8:00 in the morning, and the shop didn't open for another two hours, there—amazingly—stood the owner. Spotting us, he unlocked the door and invited us in.

When we told him that we had cancelled our plans to go digging for crystals, he replied, "What? Today is a perfect day for a dig! The rain has washed the dirt off the crystals, so they will sparkle in the sunlight and be easier to find than ever!" He convinced us that the ground was not too wet, and that, in fact, the conditions for digging were ideal.

Once again, taking what we believed to be the next right step, we turned around, drove to the mine, and had a fine day digging—unearthing more crystals in a single session than we ever had before. By 4:00 PM we were ready to call it quits. But now we had no place to stay. So what was the next right step? Should we try to check back into our hotel and spend another night in Hot Springs, as we had originally planned?

The answer seemed clear. Why kill time here? It's only 4:00 in the afternoon. By dark we could reach Memphis, Tennessee, where we could have dinner, spend the night, and be that much closer to St. Louis.

So that's what we did. And the next day—because we were now three hours closer to our final destination—we reached that riverside restaurant in time for lunch, with plenty of time left over to look through all the shops and galleries that made up the rest of the 150-year-old village.

So, was the rain a *bad* thing? Hardly. Because of the way the rain altered our plans, we not only enjoyed a great day of digging in Hot Springs, but we also experienced an interesting evening in Memphis, plus we had additional time the next day to see some sights in Missouri we otherwise would have missed. The rain, as it turned out, had been a blessing. But it was only a blessing because Carol and I successfully resisted the temptation to perceive the rain as a bad thing. Instead of letting a negative perception rule our decisions, we remained open to the flow, allowing it to tell us where to go . . . one step at a time.

Now, to be perfectly honest, when we were having breakfast in Hot Springs and the drizzle turned into a downpour, Carol and I didn't automatically jump up and down for joy, shouting, "Hooray! This must be for our highest good!" Frankly, we were very disappointed. And that's only natural. When the flow wants to take you in a direction that is different from the one you originally planned, the change can feel uncomfortable at first. But suffering over it is optional. Suffering comes from your continued resistance to seeing the situation in any other light.

I have to admit that, at an earlier time in my life, I would have suffered over that rain. I would have made a snap judgment about it, hastily thrown the bags in the car, and angrily sped out of town—perceiving the whole experience as a total disaster and stewing about it all the way to St. Louis.

If you are suffering because there is a difference between where you want to go and what seems to be the direction of the flow, once again the best advice is to let go of what you think you know. Let go of what you think your good is. Let go of how you think you have to get there. And accept what is. When you judge something as bad—when you think you know something to be true when it is only true from your imperfect point of view—you are trapped in a nightmare of your own making.

You might think at this point that I'm going to tell you to let go of your biased perception so you can transform your frightening dream— your nightmare—into a pleasant dream, instead. But I'm not, because that would only be trading one dream for another. As I have grown in my spiritual understanding I have come to believe the following. Peace is not a dream. It is real. Joy is not a dream. It is real. Goodness is not a dream. Beauty is not a dream. And love is not a dream. They are all real. These heavenly states are, in fact, the only things that *are* real. All else is an illusion—a bad dream that you can choose to wake up from at any moment.

Wake up! And see how quickly your nightmare disappears in the light of True Knowledge. It is the sure and unshakable Knowledge that you are a beloved child of God, and as such, you are never apart from the divine protection and direction of your loving Parent. The very fact that this book has been published is a testimony to what can happen when a person chooses to see a so-called bad situation in the light of Truth.

I spent more than thirty years as an advertising writer. One of the accounts at the last agency I worked for was American Airlines. Shortly after the events of September 11, 2001, American called our company to say that they were going to suspend advertising for the following quarter. Staffing cutbacks were quickly announced, and I was among the employees who were laid off.

Sure, my first reaction was fear. Without a steady income, how would I be able to pay my substantial bills? How could I afford to go to the doctor without group health insurance? And how hard would it be for me to get another job . . . especially at my age?

All of these nightmarish thoughts ran through my mind as I lay awake that first evening. But then, suddenly, I was overcome with a profound feeling of well-being. Like a ray of morning sun, it dawned on me that my layoff could be a tremendous blessing. After all, I had been laid off, not fired. That meant that I would be fortunate enough to receive some severance pay, which gave me the luxury of a choice. I could stash the cash away and immediately find another job—any job—just so I could feel secure again. Or, I could put my faith in the beneficence of the universe, and use that money to temporarily pay my bills while I pursued a desire that I had held for many years: to write this book.

The more I thought about it, the more enthusiastic I became. From the depth of my being arose the clear and certain Truth that my layoff was, indeed, a golden opportunity for me . . . *if I wanted it to be.* Was it a gift from God? Maybe. Maybe not.

On the Sunday before I was laid off, I had prayed that I would soon find a new livelihood, one that allowed me to use my communication skills to help others grow in their spiritual understanding, as I was growing in mine. Perhaps my layoff was the divine flow's direct response to my prayer—a push in the right direction. On the other hand, I had grown increasingly weary of my advertising career. My whole heart had not been in my work for quite some time. With the focus of my attention elsewhere, perhaps the loss of my job was the natural consequence of my mind-set. Who knows?

Just as it is impossible to know with complete certainty what all the next right steps will be, it is equally impossible to know with complete certainty why things happen the way they do. But the point is this. You don't have to know why anything happens. *Because it doesn't make any difference!* Regardless of where you are, regardless of how you got there, and regardless of how bad you perceive your situation to be, it can always be a stepping-stone to your highest good . . . if you are willing to look at it that way.

When that awareness dawns on you, there is no longer any reason for you to fret, fume, worry, or suffer over any circumstance you may find yourself in. You can't help but feel relieved and at peace—merry, even. And that's important.

Because as you row, row, row your boat gently down the stream, you will quickly discover that your attitude is just as important as your actions.

7

MERRILY, MERRILY,
MERRILY, MERRILY

A feeling of merriment—of cheerfulness and exuberance—occurs naturally whenever you believe that absolutely everything that happens in your life can be a portal to your highest good. As the saying goes,

> *"Everything is good in the end.*
> *If it's not good, it's not the end!"*

To row merrily, merrily, merrily, merrily means more than refusing to label something as bad. And it means more than accepting what is. To row merrily, merrily, merrily, merrily means that you are consistently choosing—time after time after time after time—to see every questionable situation as a miracle in the making and a blessing about to bloom. When you adopt this merry mind-set—this perpetually positive outlook on life—you become a channel of immeasurable creative power.

Some people call this power "the power of positive thinking." But don't confuse the word "positive" with "optimistic." Even the most optimistic person remains, if only to a small degree, somewhat uncertain. To be truly positive is to leave no room in your mind for a single shred of doubt. It means to know *without a doubt* that God is continually guiding you toward your highest good in every single circumstance, because that is the incontrovertible nature of God.

When—despite all outward appearances—you are positive that God is ceaselessly directing you toward the greatest fulfillment of your grandest dreams, there is a subtle, but significant, shift in your focus. Instead of concentrating on telling God what you want, you simply begin to concentrate on *accepting* that goodness into your life.

Are you ready to receive what you are asking for? *Honestly* ready? If you want to know how ready you really are, then pay attention to the way you express your desire in the first place.

The single most positive way to express a desire is in the form of an affirmation. An affirmation is a statement of what you know to be true in spirit. It declares that what you want (or its equivalent, or something greater) is already yours by divine right, and that you are grateful to God for its fulfillment.

An affirmation for prosperity, for instance, can be as simple as, *"I am prosperous! Thank you, God!"* Notice how this affirmation is stated in the present tense. This kind of present-tense affirmation is powerful because nothing can block your receiving when you believe, in effect, that you have already received. Nothing can prevent you from accomplishing your goal when you believe, in effect, that your goal has already been accomplished. Nothing can stand in the way of your dream when you believe, in effect, that your dream has already been realized. When, in your consciousness, what you want *already is,* you automatically think the kinds of thoughts and take the kinds of actions that lead to the manifestation of your desire in the material world. There is no greater state of openness and receptiveness to the divine flow than being positive that your every desire has already—in spirit—been fulfilled.

A less direct but still powerful affirmation for prosperity goes like this: *"I desire prosperity. And I know, God, that you desire prosperity for me, as well. Therefore, I know that prosperity is being manifested in my life right now. And I gratefully accept it. Thank you!"* This type of approach may be more realistic for you if you have trouble affirming something that your physical senses tell you does not exist at this present moment. But that doesn't mean that you should shift your focus onto the future. The only time that opportunity ever knocks is in the now. And the only time that you can ever answer that knock is in the now. So it's important to keep your awareness and your attention fully fixed in the present, letting go and allowing the divine flow to take care of the particulars.

As you can see, both of these types of affirmative prayers—for prayers are what they really are—are not meant to persuade or to convince God to give you your good. Their primary purpose is to help *you* remind *yourself* to be open and receptive to that good . . . a good that God has already guaranteed you.

Unfortunately, instead of constantly affirming the good that God has for you, chances are you limit your good by infrequently pleading with God, instead. *"Please, God, please give me this!"* you cry, but only when all else has failed and you are up against a wall. Does God hear that kind of plea? You bet. And does God answer it? Without question. The problem is, when your state of mind is one of doubt and desperation, how open and receptive to God's reply are you? Nothing interferes with your ability to follow the flow more than fear. That doesn't mean that miracles can't occur when you are fearful. It just means that miracles are more difficult for you to recognize when your perception of reality is clouded or shrouded by anxiety or apprehension.

An even more restrictive expression of desire comes in the form of a negation—a negative affirmation, if you will. In your desperate desire for prosperity, for example, you may say something like, *"I never have enough money!"* Fortunately, God looks beneath this kind of negative statement, sees the true underlying desire for prosperity, and begins to fulfill that desire in the most beneficial way possible. With your negative mind-set, however, the likelihood of you accepting God's generous gift is slim or none, because there is virtually no openness or receptiveness on your part. Your mind is already closed. And with your mind closed, your ears and eyes are closed, as well. You cannot hear what your intuition is trying to tell you. You cannot see what the signs are trying to show you. You cannot follow the flow because you have mentally and emotionally cut yourself off from G.O.D.—the Guidance Of the Divine. As a result of this kind of self-sabotage, your desire—exactly as you stated it—is likely to become a self-fulfilling prophecy. You never have enough money!

And then there is this kind of negative statement: *"I'd like to change careers, but I can't because there's just no money in what I really want to do."* In this case, you have shut the door on one desire—your dream job—by deciding that another desire—prosperity—cannot come to you through that particular avenue. How do you know that it can't? And why do you think that it has to? Do you really believe that God is so limited that God simply cannot grant you—in some unforeseen manner—both prosperity *and* a fulfilling career? Well, if that's what you think, then God can't! Remember, the divine flow doesn't deliver the fulfillment of your desires *to* you, as much as it delivers it *through* you—through the God-guided decisions that you make and through the divinely inspired steps that you take. Once again, the issue here is not about God's willingness to hear and grant your request. It's about your willingness to be open and receptive to God's response.

It is important to always remember that the power of positive thinking doesn't depend solely on how effective a *transmitter* you are. To a considerable degree, the power of positive thinking depends on how highly sensitive a *receiver* you are. In that sense, you are very much—as I stated earlier—a channel of creativity. You are continuously *sending* messages to God, yes. But you are also simultaneously *receiving* messages from God. Whenever you are being negative instead of positive—whenever you are gripped by worry or concern, negating your good, or restricting it in some way—you are crimping that channel. You are sending out a weak signal, a mixed signal, or no signal at all.

And at the same time, you are seriously limiting your ability to pick up any signals that the universe may be sending you.

Do you see what this suggests? It suggests that negativity is not the power to create negatively. It is only a self-induced *reduction* in your God-given power to create positively. To me, that means that negativity has no real power of its own. Not a little power. Not a lesser power. *No* power. None.

When you consistently entertain negative thoughts, yes, life can be more difficult than it is divinely designed to be. Getting to your good can be effortful and fraught with unexpected obstacles. But it is not because you are wielding some kind of anti-positive power.

The way I see it—and I admit that it may just be a matter of semantics—you do not have the power to literally *attract* trouble into your life through some kind of negative magnetic force. You do not have the power to literally *draw* unwelcome circumstances to you. However, when you let doubt and dread rule your head—when you row without the help of the flow, consciously or unconsciously forgoing divine direction—there can certainly be undesirable consequences.

It's like trying to make your way across an unfamiliar room in the middle of the night. Without a guiding light, it's almost impossible to avoid bumping into something. But you did not *draw* that something to you. You simply ran into it because you couldn't see it in the darkness. You did not *attract* a collision. You were simply more susceptible to a collision as the natural result of your blindness.

This susceptibility, I believe, is the main reason that so-called bad things happen to so-called good people. Most of us are not walking around totally in the dark, that is, completely cut off from the light of God. But most of us are not walking around totally in the light, either. Most of us go through our daily lives in a kind of twilight. We're not necessarily self-destructive, but we're certainly not consciously constructive, either. We're somewhere in between. We *sort of* tell God what we want, and we *sort of* listen to what God has to say. We pay just enough attention to avoid *some* problems, but in the dimness that is caused by fear, inattention, distraction, or distrust, we run right smack dab into *other* problems . . . sometimes with devastating results for ourselves, and for all involved.

Don't allow an already dim light to become even dimmer by fearing the power of negativity. It has no power. Whenever you find yourself stumbling around in the night, just turn on the light! Spend a few moments in prayer and meditation, to consciously reconnect to the one and only light that can offer you protection through its direction. It is the light that illuminates your path by illuminating your mind. It is the light of God within you. It is the light of God that *is* you. It is the light of your holy spirit . . . a light that shines deeply within your own heart.

Whenever you connect to that inner light—that *heart* light—you immediately improve your ability to discern the next right step to take. And you improve something else, as well . . . something that is equally important. You improve your immediate sense of well-being. You become—to use a play on words—*light*hearted! This light-heartedness can range from a simple sense of peace to a profound experience of joy.

Peace is what you feel when you connect to your spirit in its most fundamental state—at rest in its oneness with God. Commonly experienced in times of prayer and meditation, this abiding sense of serenity and security originates from a place that's beyond time and space—a place that's beyond the body and beyond the physical world that the body lives in.

Joy, on the other hand, is the innate state of your *embodied* spirit. It arises from the fact that—even in the body—your spirit never senses any separation from the presence of God, the power of God, the guidance of God, and most importantly, the unconditional love of God. So, like a child at play in the care of a trusted parent, your spirit always feels happily protected. The French call this kind of happiness *joie de vivre,* the joy of life. It is the joy of just being alive and in the world. And it's what you feel whenever you express *in the body* the truth of who you are *in spirit.*

As you can see, then, to row merrily, merrily, merrily, merrily means a whole lot more than just maintaining a positive attitude. It means more than being positive that your good is always at hand. And it means more than knowing that to receive that good, all you have to do is accept it into your life.

To row merrily, merrily, merrily, merrily is to understand that ultimately—as good as your good may be—your happiness does not depend upon manifesting that good. It is to recognize that *real* happiness—true, long-lasting happiness—comes from within. It is something that you *already* possess, and can always access, at the core of your being.

To row merrily, merrily, merrily, merrily is to know that nothing outside of yourself has the power to make you happy—nothing that you acquire, and nothing that you achieve. Happiness is fundamentally a choice. It is something that you *allow* yourself to feel, and something that can only come from that innately joyful place within you. And in the end, as it is in the beginning, it is that abiding *inner joy* that enables you to *enjoy* this journey we call life.

8

LIFE

Early on in this book, you may have gotten the impression that the reason you pick a destination and row toward it is so you can be happy once you get there—once you attain your goal or realize your dream. But I hope you are now beginning to see that you don't have to arrive anywhere in life in order to be happy. Happiness is something that can be experienced *right where you are,* whenever you remember *who you are*—God's own protected and privileged child.

But that raises an interesting question. If happiness is inherent—if the source of happiness is an inner one rather than an outer one—then what's the point of choosing a destination and rowing toward it? I'd like to answer that question with two more questions. What happens when you put a happy child on a playground? Doesn't he or she immediately run to the nearest swing, sandbox, seesaw, or slide, and begin to play?

To your spirit—that joyful child within you—the material world is one big playground under God's watchful eye. And it is only natural for a safe and happy child to want to enjoy the world that it finds itself in . . . to want to ride on the merry-go-round, to want to climb on the monkey bars, to want to sing, dance, paint, write, go to the movies and eat a big bag of popcorn . . . to *want,* period!

In other words, it is in your very nature for you to have desires, and for you to row, row, row your boat in pursuit of their fulfillment. Even the genesis of the word "desire" supports this idea. If you look up "desire" in the dictionary, you will see that it developed from a combination of the Latin words *de* and *sidus,* which translate literally as "from a star." Desire, then, is not a human failing (or falling). Far from it! Desire in its purest form is a *heavenly* attribute, one born from that higher place—that higher self—that star that is your spirit.

Do you have a desire in mind? Is there somewhere that you want to go? Then pick up your oars and row! But don't make the mistake of putting off your happiness until you get there. Remember, the happiness you feel when you get where you want to go is just the icing on the cake. The real, deep-down enjoyment of life comes from allowing yourself to appreciate every moment of the trip, not just your arrival at a particular point.

Whether you are building a home, raising a family, or launching a career, consciously choose to savor each and every second of that experience, not just the milestones. As so many have said before me:

> *"Life is not about the destination.*
> *It's about the journey!"*

Of course, it's easy to enjoy that journey when it seems like everything is going your way. And I do believe that the more you practice rowing with the flow, the more life *will* go your way. Miracles will abound and obstacles will dissolve, as you learn how to let go and let God guide you to your greatest good. But can I guarantee you that you will never again row your boat into the rocks? No.

As I have said, as long as you and every other child of God have the divine right to choose freely, life can—and undoubtedly will—have its challenges. Your conscious and unconscious freewill choices, combined with the conscious and unconscious freewill choices of others, can quickly carry you out of the flow and into some fairly undesirable situations.

That's not a problem if you are willing to look at those situations in a positive light, though, right? Right. It's not a problem at all . . . as long as you are also willing to look at everyone involved in those situations in the same positive light. Are you?

One of the most important things to know about rowing with the flow is this: to see the good that lies within a situation, you must also see the good that lies within each and every person involved in that situation—especially anyone you are blaming for bringing that situation about. You cannot judge or hold a grudge, and, at the same time, be open and receptive to God's guidance and God's gifts.

To row with the flow, you have to release your resentments and give up your judgments. In short—you have to love! Fortunately, like pursuing a desire or expressing your joy, loving others is one of the most natural things in the world for you to do. In fact, love is not only *in* your nature, it *is* your nature. How so?

If you believe, as I do, that the energy of God is a loving energy, and that your spirit is an individual expression of that energy, then God is love, and so is your spirit! That is why I said in the very first chapter of this book that your spirit is the *heart* of your boat.

To love is to come from your heart instead of your head. It is to express who you truly are *at heart* . . . love itself! And more than that, to love is to recognize that all others have that same loving spirit within them. To love is to look beyond a person's outward appearance to behold the inner perfection, the inner innocence, and the inner glory that comprise his or her true nature. Carol put it very poetically when she said:

> *"To see with the eyes*
> *is to see only in part.*
> *To see the whole, you must*
> *look from the heart."*

A friend of mine named Hami is a good example of someone who consistently sees others in this loving way. Hami was one of the first people I met at the church that was my spiritual home from 1994 to 2006. Right from the start, she seemed to go out of her way to compliment me, commend me, and thank me for the many ways in which I was helping her to grow spiritually. On one level I appreciated her praise and gratefulness, but on another level I didn't feel completely worthy of it because I was very much aware of my many human foibles and failings.

One afternoon, right after Hami had honored me once again, I replied to her, "You know, Hami, you might not say such nice things to me if you *really knew me.*" And then, just as quickly as I had said it, I took it back. For it instantly occurred to me that Hami was one of the few people in the world who *really did know me*— because Hami *knew my spirit!* Hami was well aware of my human shortcomings, as was I. But she chose to acknowledge only my authentic nature . . . the caring and creative being within me . . . the being that is loving in nature and infinite in potential. Hami respected my humanity. But what she actively embraced was my divinity. And you know what? With that kind of loving support, it was easy for me to be exactly the kind of person that she was praising me for being.

To practice love in this manner is to understand love as a state of being rather than a way of feeling. You are, in a very real sense, love incarnate. And as love incarnate, it serves you well to be the love that you are in every single circumstance—yes, even when you perceive that you have been attacked in some way. To love in response to a perceived offense is usually referred to as forgiveness. But allow me to clear up a common misconception about forgiveness.

Forgiveness is not, as some assume, about condoning unproductive or destructive behavior. It is not about letting someone off the hook. There is nothing wrong with holding someone accountable for his or her irresponsible actions, and taking whatever steps are required to protect yourself and all others from future injury.

Forgiveness is simply about making a distinction between a person's behavior and the truth of who that person is in spirit. To forgive is to see every person in the world as a holy child of

God, doing the best he or she can with the limited knowledge and imperfect understanding that he or she has. It is to recognize how easy it is for anyone and everyone—including yourself—to forget their connection to God, to fall into fear, and to make choices based on that fear that are harmful to themselves and to others . . . to attack, control, betray, cheat, lie, and steal. As deeply buried as a person's spiritual essence may be, to forgive is to recognize and honor that person's spirit . . . *anyway!* It is to love them . . . *anyway!*

The next time you need to look on the bright side of a situation, don't forget to look on the bright side of everyone associated with that situation. Look upon the *brightness* that is *inside* them! When you do, you will be amazed at the miracles that will follow. A small business challenge I faced a few years ago clearly illustrated for me the benefits of looking at a situation through the eyes of love.

My challenge began when I awoke one night in a state of extreme anxiety. I had an important presentation to make the next morning to the president of my advertising agency. I was supposed to show him three television commercials that I had written for one of our most important clients, and I was convinced that he wasn't going to approve all of my scripts. That would mean big trouble for me because our client was expecting to see my ideas by noon that same day.

My mind raced with thoughts about how opinionated the president of my agency could be and how demanding our client usually was. I fretted over the unusually tight timetable. And I even began to doubt the quality of my own work. As I lay in bed second-guessing myself and everyone else, I became certain of one thing, and one thing only. I no longer wanted to feel the way I was feeling.

At that moment, I became sincerely willing to see the situation differently—to look at it from a higher perspective. And that little bit of willingness was all it took for me to suddenly see things in a whole new light . . . a much more loving light . . . a light that instantly revealed to me the real truth of the matter.

For one, I saw that my fear was completely self-inflicted because what I feared had not actually happened, nor was there any way of knowing that it actually *would* happen. I realized that I was guilty of doing what so many of us do so much of the time—I was experiencing in my mind something that had not yet happened in my life, and might not happen at all. I was living in a made-up future, and I was completely missing the serenity and tranquility that existed for me in the current moment—in the still of the night and in the warmth of my bed.

I also saw that I was harshly judging myself, the president of my agency, and our client. My fears were based on the assumptions that my work was somehow inferior, and that the president of my agency and our client were both looking for ways to reject what I had done. But what was the actual truth? What was the Truth with a capital T?

As I looked beyond my fear-based percep-
tions and peered into the hearts of all involved, I
quickly realized that we were all one in spirit, and
that in spirit we all wanted the exact same thing.
The client wanted three good commercials.
That's all. The president of my agency wanted
three good commercials. That's all. And I wanted
three good commercials. That's all. No one was
intentionally trying to undermine my efforts. The
exact opposite was true. In spirit, each of us
wanted to reach the same destination, and we
were all working together to do just that.

With this new vision of reality firmly seated
in my mind, I immediately regained my sense of
inner peace, and I was quickly able to drift back
to sleep. The next morning I awoke with a joyful
sense of anticipation, and I went to see the president of my agency with a much more positive
attitude. Was I positive that he would approve all
of my scripts? Not at all. What I was positive
about was this: that everything would work out in
a way that was the best for all concerned, as long

as I maintained an open mind and an open heart. And that's exactly what happened.

Although the president of my agency approved my first two scripts right off the bat, he rejected the third one. Believe me, in the past I would have taken his disapproval personally and defended my work vehemently. And worse, I would have completely panicked about how I was going to come up with a new script in time to make my noon meeting with the client. Instead, with my newfound sense of spiritual security and surety, what could have been a battle of egos became nothing more than an enjoyable discussion.

Within minutes, the president mentioned something that caused me to recall an idea of mine that I had never been able to develop satisfactorily. When I described the concept to him, he grew excited about it. So we talked about it for a few more seconds, and the next thing I knew, a fully formed commercial suddenly appeared in my mind.

Energized and inspired, I raced back to my

office and wrote the entire script in less than three minutes. The president enthusiastically approved it. The client appreciatively received it. And along with my other two scripts, all three commercials were produced and aired, and they generated excellent sales results.

For me, the way things unfolded so easily, so effortlessly, and to everyone's mutual benefit was a great demonstration of the flow in action. And it helped me understand how vital love is when it comes to living life in the divine flow. This experience and many others have taught me that love enhances your ability to row with the flow in four very practical and very powerful ways.

~ One ~
LOVE CONNECTS YOU
TO YOUR INNER GUIDANCE

Throughout this book I have repeatedly mentioned the importance of following your intuition. Well, since the source of your intuition is your spirit, and since your spirit is love itself, then it follows that when you express love you are opening up a channel for the inspiration and insight of your spirit to make its way into the world. It is through love that you are ultimately connected to the source of all wisdom—God. And it is through love that your conscious mind becomes a receptive and fertile ground for divine ideas to take hold and grow.

So, if you want to be in the flow from the very start, get out of your head and into your heart. Let go of what you think you know about any unwelcome situation that you encounter, and let go of what you think you know about anyone involved in that situation. Let go of all those mental judgments and resulting resentments that are blocking your ability to hear what your heart is trying to tell you.

~ Two ~
LOVE BRINGS OUT
THE WISDOM IN OTHERS

Do you recall what I said in chapter 3 about God's unending efforts to communicate with you? I said that "God is always—and in all ways—showing you the next right step to take." And do you recall what I said was one of the most common ways that God speaks to you (other than through your own intuition)? I said that it is "through the people who are put in your path." So, one of the main ways that you receive guidance from God is through the God-given messages that people are divinely inspired to deliver to you. These messages—these directions—come directly from their spirit . . . their God-self. But if an individual does not feel safe—if he or she feels threatened by you for any reason—then his or her conscious connection to that higher self may become severed by fear, and the message cannot be delivered.

If you want to follow the flow, then, it is not only kind, but it is also wise to treat all the people who cross your path with the compassion, understanding, and respect that they deserve as

your brothers and sisters in spirit. Create a supportive environment that encourages their inner
light to shine. Uplift them with your love and free
them to express their higher selves. There is no
guarantee that they will take that opportunity
and rise to the occasion. But I can guarantee you
this: If you judge them for any reason—any reason at all—odds are they will *not* be able to
pass along any word of God that they may have
for you. Nor will you—coming from your head
instead of your heart—be able to pass along any
word of God that you may have for them.

~ Three ~
LOVE TRANSFORMS

Although I personally believe that love is a
true power—in fact, the *only* power—and that
the power of love can produce a miraculous shift
in circumstances, in many cases love does
not outwardly change anything at all. What love
does do, however, and does consistently, is return

everyone involved in those circumstances to their naturally creative, cooperative, wise, and joyful states. And *that* creates the kind of atmosphere in which a change in circumstances not only becomes possible, it becomes probable!

Just think about it. How can a situation that began with fear and false assumptions, mistrust and misperceptions, *not* begin to change for the better when you begin to express the love that you are in that situation, and in response, others feel safe enough to express the love that they are? How can a situation *not* begin to change for the better when people start to honor each other's spirits, and begin to communicate with each other in mutually supportive and constructive ways? How can a situation *not* begin to change for the better when everyone involved in that situation becomes divinely directed?

Whenever you allow love to lead the way, you are in the flow. And the flow has a wonderful way of transforming dead-end tributaries into perfect passageways to good—not necessarily by transforming situations themselves, but by transforming the way that you respond to those situations. And if the only thing about a situation that changes for the better is the way that you feel about it? That's enough! Which brings us to the final and most important benefit of love:

~ Four ~
LOVE FEELS GOOD!

As I said at the end of the last chapter, "Joy is what you feel whenever you express in the body the truth of who you are in spirit." Well, who you are in spirit is love. So when you express love, you feel joy!

Many believe that *being loved* is what feels good, but that's only how it appears. The fact is, when someone extends love to you, you don't automatically feel good. What you feel is safe enough to love them back. And loving them back is what feels good. It is *being love*—not *being loved*—that is the real source of your joy.

Conversely, when you perceive that someone is attacking you, it's not what he or she is doing that makes you feel bad. What feels bad is judging them instead of loving them. It's *not* being yourself—*not* being the love that you are—that is the real source of your unhappiness.

When you experience the joy that comes from loving, you experience one of life's greatest truths: the truth that *love is its own reward.* When you love, life is so satisfying, so gratifying, so meaningful and rewarding, it doesn't make one bit of difference where you are along the course of the stream—whether you are just about to reach your dream, or whether you are still miles away from it.

Does that mean that all of your goals, your plans, your aims and aspirations become irrelevant? Not in the least. As I have already explained, it is in your very nature for you to have desires, and for you to row, row, row your boat in pursuit of their fulfillment. What *does* become irrelevant is the actual *outcome* of your pursuit, because you know that your happiness does not rely on what that outcome is.

When you express love, life is good just the way it is, and you are happy—right where you are, wherever you are. And when all is said and done, isn't happiness all that you really want out of life? Isn't happiness all that you really need out of life? Isn't happiness all that God has been trying to help you get out of life . . . all along?

So, dear reader, go ahead and choose a destination. Pick up your oars and begin to row, row, row your boat gently down the stream. With God as your guide, you can be positive that the divine flow will lead you to your highest good with effortless ease. But more importantly, with God *inside,* you will understand that your arrival at your chosen destination is not, nor has it ever been, what the journey of life is all about.

The journey of life is not about *getting somewhere.* The journey of life is about *being something.* It's about being the love that you are in every single moment of that journey. And it's about experiencing the absolute joy that your love brings to the journey, and brings to each and every spirit that you encounter along the way.

Here's to a joyful, effortless, and fulfilling journey, my friend. Bon voyage! And Godspeed!

Author's Note

≈

As I mentioned in the Preface to this book, my first introduction to the divine flow was more than twenty years ago—1985, to be exact. It was not until ten years later that I recognized the parallel between the principles of going with the flow and the lyrics to *Row, Row, Row Your Boat*. The correlation between the two suddenly occurred to me while I was driving down the highway one Sunday after church.

I was so excited by this association that I immediately began to use this rich, spiritual metaphor as the basis for various talks that I have been presenting since 1995. In December of 2001, I finally began to put my ideas on paper.

And the result is the book you are reading now—a book that is currently in its third printing.

Since completing this book, I have discovered that I am not the only person to have been inspired by *Row, Row, Row Your Boat*. Over the years, many others have formulated their own explanations of its lyrics—including noted speaker and author, Dr. Wayne Dyer. I have no doubt that many more insights can be gained from a study of this popular piece. Perhaps you will discover a few yourself. These pages offer only my own interpretation of this cherished old song, and what it uniquely means to me.

STEVEN LANE TAYLOR
MAY, 2008

ACKNOWLEDGMENT

When I began working on this book, my partner, Carol, said to me, "You know, Steve, you're going to have to live this book as you write it." Truer words were never spoken. Even though I have been teaching the principles contained in *Row, Row, Row Your Boat* for many years, I discovered that when I tried to commit them to the written word, the flow would direct me in one way or another to experience the truth of what I was writing about.

Sometimes these experiences would confirm a concept that I had long held to be true. Other times they would clarify a point that I had come to find contradictory or confusing. And still other times these experiences would lead me to a higher truth that was altogether new to me.

With each paragraph—each line, some-times—I felt as if I was being guided by the flow to a deeper understanding of it. In fact, the entire writing process itself turned out to be a wonder-ful lesson in learning how to row with the flow. I can't tell you the number of times I felt like I had written myself into a corner and then had to let go and allow the flow to lead me in a new direc-tion. Sometimes it took a day, sometimes two days, sometimes three, but always within a rel-atively short amount of time I would receive from my inner spirit a brand-new insight that solved my problem and guided me onward.

And then an even bigger miracle would occur. Invariably, someone I did not know, or a book I had not read, would immediately cross my path and, in one way or another, clearly corroborate, substantiate, or support the direction I had received from within. My confidence was bol-stered, my enthusiasm renewed.

Needless to say, with each demonstration of the flow—and the inspiration and revelation that came with it—my sense of gratitude for the flow grew greatly. To that end, I wish to express my heartfelt appreciation to the divine flow for the opportunity it gave me to write this book, for the invaluable help it freely offered me while I was writing it, and for the assistance it provided me in getting it published. But most of all, I wish to thank the divine flow for the joy, peace, and prosperity that it blesses me with each and every day . . . and for all the loving and supportive people that the flow has had me encounter along the way.

Thank you . . . God.